Sydney Kangaroo

Malachy Doyle
Illustrated by Delphine Thomas

Sydney was born in the red dust of the Australian bush. As soon as he was born, he climbed up his mother's fur towards her pouch and climbed inside. He felt safe and warm in there.

Sydney stayed in his mother's pouch for many months.

He grew bigger, and his back legs and tail grew longer. Soft grey fur grew all over him. His ears became pointed, just like his mother's.

Then, one day, Sydney was big enough to peep out of the pouch. The bright light made him blink as he felt the warm sun for the first time. A gentle breeze tickled his face.

Sydney watched his mother bend down to eat grass. Sydney tried to eat some, too. The next thing he knew, he was rolling on the ground and his mother was looking down at him.

He had tumbled out of her pouch!

As Sydney got older, he spent more and more time out of the pouch. He learned to hop and jump, springing into the air with his strong back legs.

"Well done, Sydney," said his mother, proudly. "You will grow up to be a big, strong kangaroo."

One warm afternoon, Sydney and his mother went looking for some fresh, tasty grass to eat. Suddenly his mother's nose twitched.

"Dingoes!" she hissed, sniffing the air. Sydney looked up, frightened.

In the distance he could see a band of wild dogs – dingoes! They looked fierce and hungry. Sydney dived into his mother's pouch. He trembled when he heard the dogs begin to howl.

Sydney's mother stood still. She hoped the hungry dingoes would not see or smell her. But they came closer and closer, until she knew she had to get away.

"Hold tight," she whispered to Sydney. Then, with great flying leaps, she bounded away through the bushes. Sydney was afraid he might fall out, but his mother had tightened her pouch, so he was safe.

Sydney peeped out and saw the dingoes close behind, howling and snarling.

"Run, Mother, run!" he cried.

Sydney's mother ran as fast as she could but she soon grew tired. She knew she would have to stand and fight.

The dingoes closed in on her, trying to bite. She kicked them and scratched them, and kept them away from little Sydney.

Just then, a great buck kangaroo appeared. He was a giant of a kangaroo, with a creamy chest and a broad, red back. He thumped his tail on the ground when he saw the dingoes, and then he leaped at them. The dingoes were so frightened of the great buck that they ran away.

Then the great buck smiled at Sydney and bounded off into the haze of the late afternoon.

In the cool of the evening, Sydney curled up in his mother's pouch, safe again.

"Soon I'll be too big for your pouch, Mother," said Sydney.

"Yes, soon you'll be a big, strong kangaroo, just like the great buck," replied his mother.

Sydney closed his eyes, went to sleep, and dreamed about fighting dingoes.